SPUNKY SCIENCE

COLORING BOOKS

available at

amazon

SPUNKY SCIENCE

WHAT'S IN THE BOOK?

- Winter word find
- How's the weather ⛄ at santa's workshop?
- Gravity in a Globe
- Nutcracker physics
- Hot cocoa heat transfer
- Christmas 🎄 tree water cycle
- Oh chemistree
- North Pole food web
- Elf on the shelf respiratory system
- Energy in a lightbulb 💡
- How snowflakes are made
- Nutrients for santa
- What is a cold front?
- Will it snow?
- Reindeer Adaptations
- Chestnuts 🌰 roasting on an open fire
- Santa's digestion
- Cells of holly
- Cells of santa 🎅
- Goat coal?
- Mammal tracks dichotomous key
- Electromagnetic spectrum- waves of the holidays
- Taxonomic classification of emperor penguin 🐧
- How does a thermometer work?
  Why do leaves change color?

WINTER

Word Find

```
A L F K T E E M N O L L O H F A M S S
J Q H I R A S N O N F E H L I J Q A N
V M N X L S L W H O T C O C O A M U I
Y G O N B J M D E A O Q F G K R J S U
L I E U K O T N S T N I C K H C A O T
W E L M F C F L O N G F D I A N L M Y
D A N O P E L F Z G O E M C E D V O N
B F B Y Z P G H F I P W C L B H P B O
C G T X H A C P L R H F A M I L Y W P
T D E Q R I T D V C O B F K A C I Q X
S T H G I L J U W Q A S B G Z R J O I
W S U B T J U K X V Z Y T R Q C U Y D
Z I N V C W E R T K W X W I N T E R B
Y A C H R I S T M A S T A S S R H E Y
```

WORDBANK

- Noel
- Holly
- St Nick
- Elf
- Frost
- snow
- Christmas
- Family
- Winter
- Lights
- Hot cocoa
- Joy

How's the weather at SANTA'S WORKSHOP?

LOCATION: NORTH POLE, ALASKA United States

BIOME: Arctic Tundra

Snows from October to April

WILDLIFE: Caribou, hares, squirrels, birds, fish, and lichens.

Daylight hours ranges from 3.5hrs in December to 21hrs in June

Toys & Joy made Here

Temperature ranges from -14 to 73

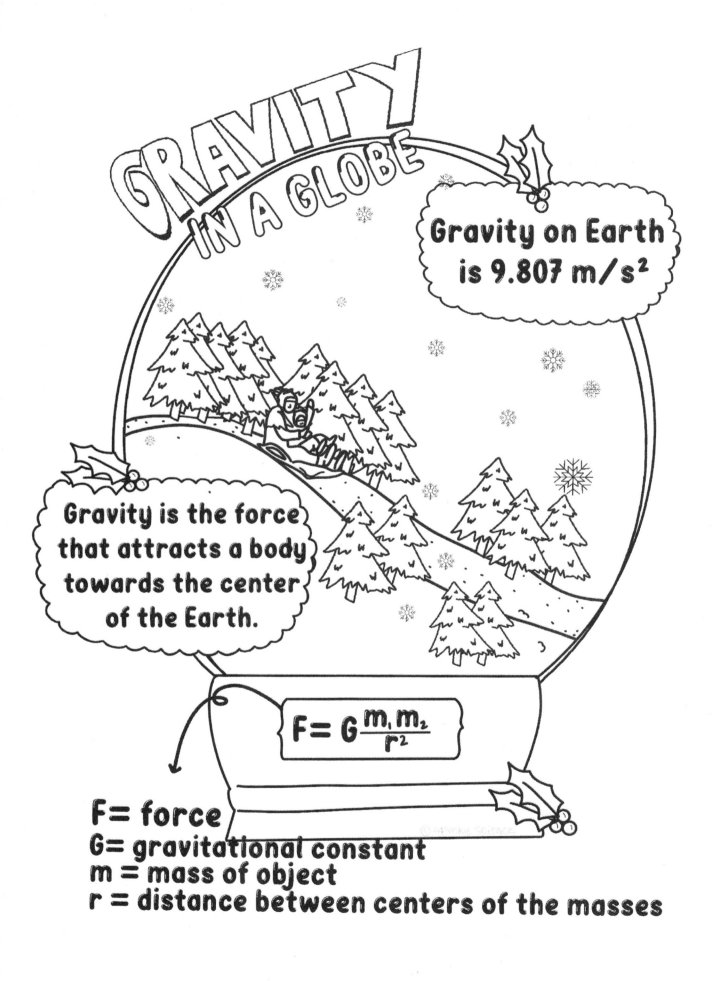

GRAVITY IN A GLOBE

Gravity on Earth is 9.807 m/s²

Gravity is the force that attracts a body towards the center of the Earth.

$$F = G\frac{m_1 m_2}{r^2}$$

F = force
G = gravitational constant
m = mass of object
r = distance between centers of the masses

NUTCRACKER PHYSICS

SECOND-CLASS LEVER

Second-class levers have a longer effort arm. This means that they can overcome heavy loads with little effort.

Load

THE NUTCRACKER REDUCES THE EFFORT NEEDED TO CRACK THE NUT

The point of a simple machine is to reduce the effort (force) needed to do the work.

effort

MECHANICAL ADVANTAGE = LOAD DIVIDED BY EFFORT.

A good mechanical advantage is above one.

FULCRUM

The fulcrum is the point on which the lever rest or is supported and on which it pivots.

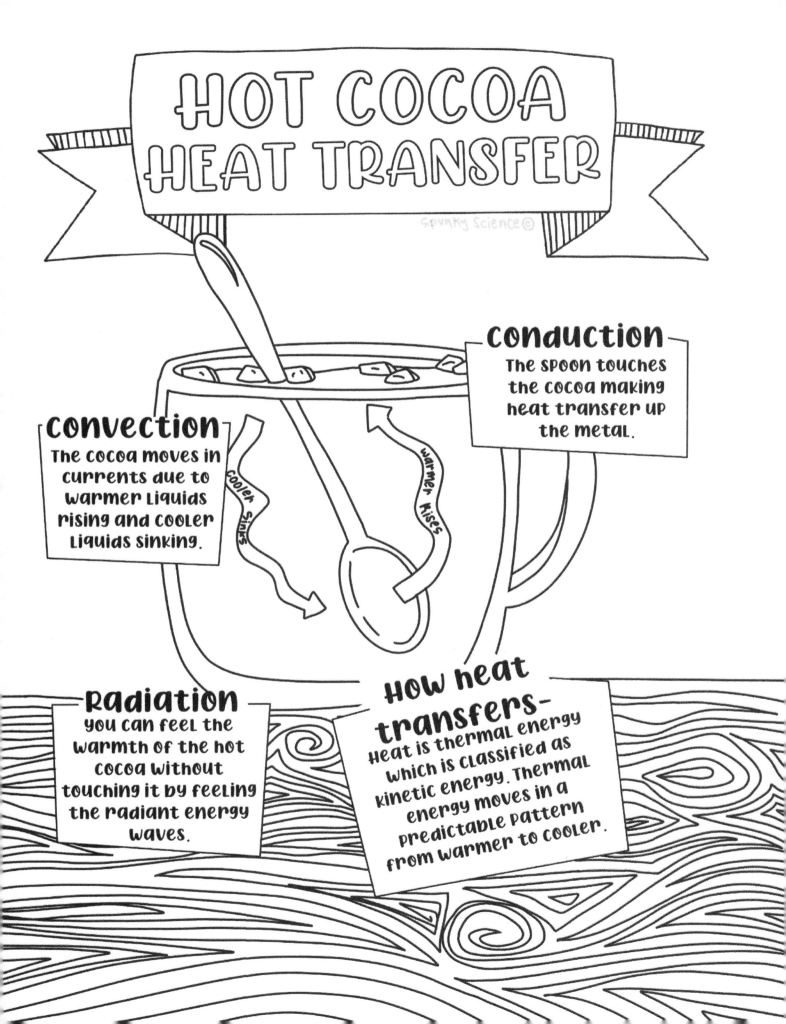

Oh Chemistree

COLOR CODE KEY
- ☐ METALS
- ☐ NON METALS
- ☐ METALLOIDS

H

He Li Be

B C N O F

Ne Na Mg Al Si

There are actually 118 elements on the Periodic Table
-Spunky Science ©

P S Cl Ar K Ca Sc

Ti V Cr Mn Fe Co Ni

Cu Zn Ga Ge As Se Br Kr Rb

Sr Y Zr Nb Mo Tc Ru Rh Pd Ag Cd

In Sn Sb Te I Xe Cs Ba La Hf Ta

W Re Os Ir Pt Au Hg Ti Pb Bi Po

At Rn Fr

Ra Ac Rf

Db Sg Bh Hs Mt Ds Rg Cn Nh Fl Mc

Lv Ts Og La Ce Pr Nd Pm Sm Eu Gd

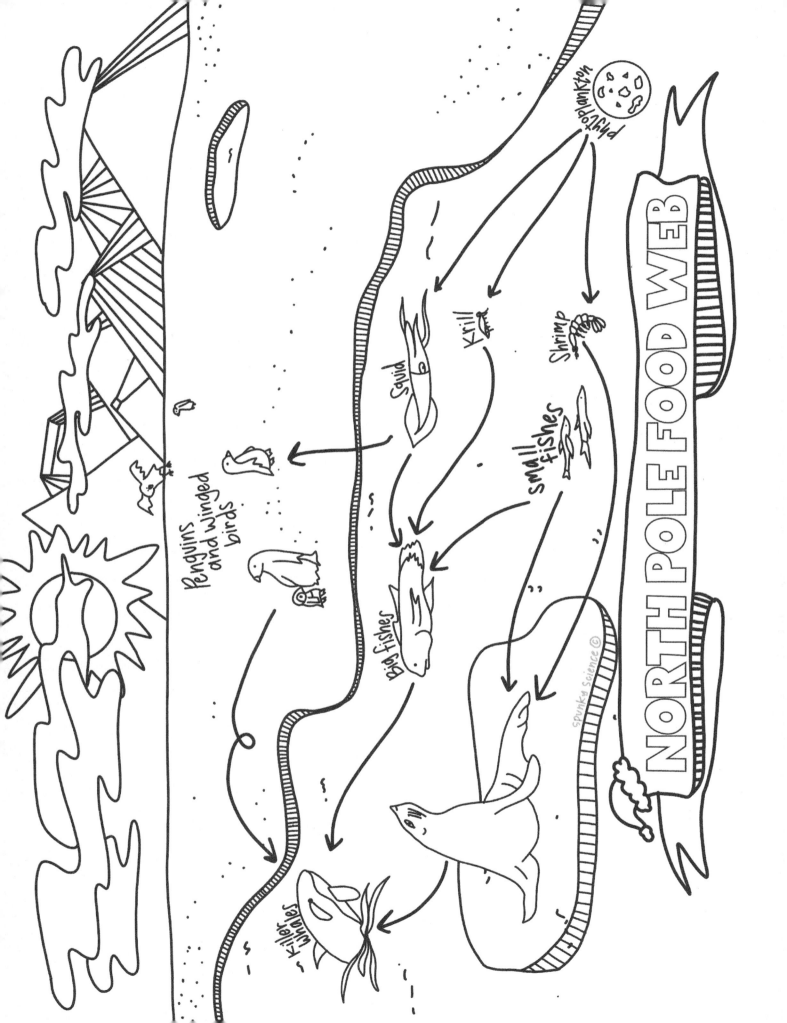

HOW SNOWFLAKES ARE MADE

Dust grain floating in air

Water vapor sticks to the dust grain

Droplets turn into ice

Prism forms with 6 faces

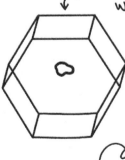

A cavity forms in each prism face

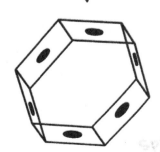

As the temperature changes, the branches grow. If it runs into warmer air, the tips get longer.

At 9°F new growth at the tips creating branches

NUTRIENTS FOR SANTA

© Spunky Science

MILK for SANTA

NUTRITIONAL FACTS

CALORIES

CHOCOLATE CHIP COOKIES ARE HIGH IN SUGAR, FATS, AND IRON.

MILK IS A GREAT SOURCE OF POTASSIUM, PROTEIN, AND CALCIUM.

NUTRITIONAL FACTS

CALORIES

What is a COLD FRONT?

Cold air

Warm air

A cold front occurs when a cold air mass pushes into a warm air mass. As a cold front moves in, the heavier (more dense) cool air pushes under the lighter (less dense) warm air causing it to rise up into the troposphere.

REINDEER ADAPTATIONS

All of Santa's reindeer are female. Males shed their antlers in early December while females keep theirs until Spring.

Specialized circulatory system helps keep the core warm.

Their noses are specially designed to warm the air before it enters their lungs.

Can run up to 45mph

Hooves are shaped to be used for paddling when swimming. They also have hair on the bottom to prevent slipping on snow.

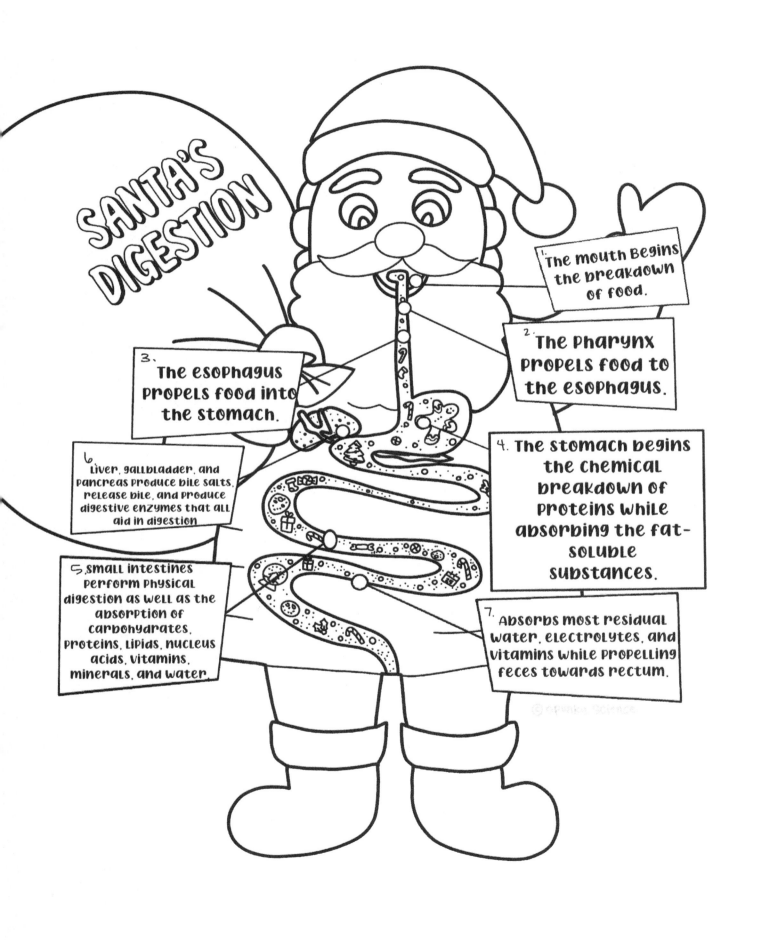

SANTA'S DIGESTION

1. The mouth Begins the breakdown of food.

2. The Pharynx Propels food to the esophagus.

3. The esophagus Propels food into the stomach.

4. The stomach begins the chemical breakdown of Proteins while absorbing the fat-soluble substances.

5. small intestines Perform Physical digestion as well as the absorption of carbohydrates, Proteins, LiPids, nucleus acids, vitamins, minerals, and water.

6. Liver, gallbladder, and Pancreas Produce bile salts, release bile, and Produce digestive enzymes that all aid in digestion

7. Absorbs most residual water, electrolytes, and vitamins while ProPelling feces towards rectum.

CELLS OF HOLLY

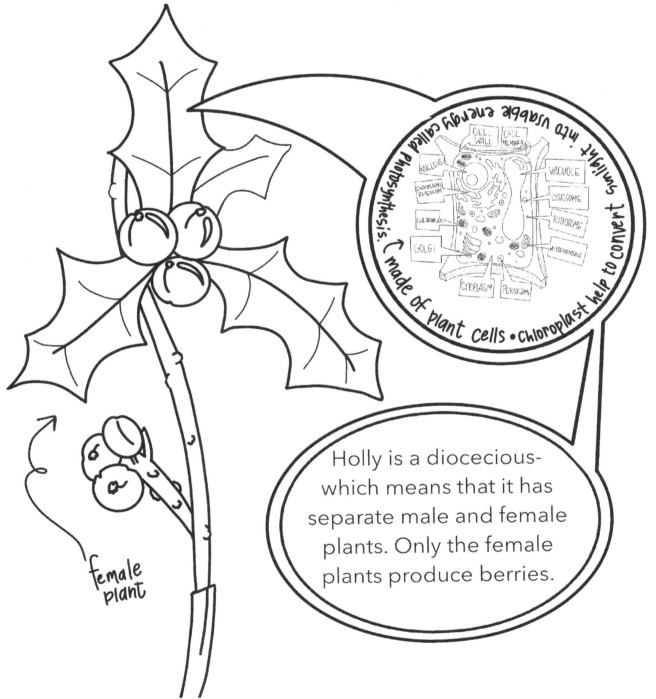

made of plant cells • Chloroplast help to convert sunlight into usable energy called photosynthesis. (

CELL WALL

CELL MEMBRANE

NUCLEUS

ENDOPLASMIC RETICULUM

CHLOROPLAST

GOLGI

CYTOPLASM

PEROXISOM

VACUOLE

LYSOSOME

RIBOSOME

MITOCHONDRIA

Holly is a diocecious- which means that it has separate male and female plants. Only the female plants produce berries.

female plant

GOT COAL?

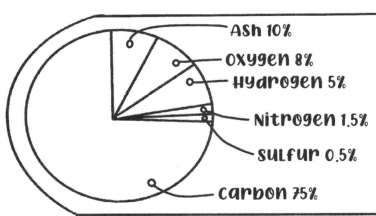

Ash 10%
Oxygen 8%
Hydrogen 5%
Nitrogen 1.5%
Sulfur 0.5%
Carbon 75%

Stats

Non renewable
sedimentary rock
Four different kinds
Formed from heat and
pressure over dead
plants.

Coal is ranked
into 4 different
categories based on
how much carbon
it has
in it.

You've been naughty
Here's your
coal

Spunky Science

Mammal Tracks
Dichotomous Key

A dichotomous key is a tool used to easily identify different organisms by their characteristics. Use the dichotomous key below to identify all 4 sets of tracks found in the snow!

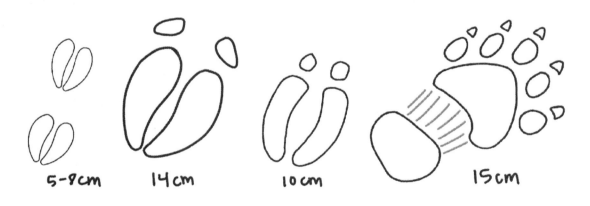

5-9cm   14cm   10cm   15cm

steps	CHARACTERISTICS	Where to go next
1	Has 2 toes per foot Has more than 2 toes per foot	Go to step 2 Bear
2	Has dew claw No dew claw	Go to step 3 Deer
3	Track is larger than 12cm Track is smaller than 12cm	Moose Caribou

ELECTROMAGNETIC SPECTRUM
WAVES OF THE HOLIDAYS

Northern lights

Neutron stars emit gamma rays

Space heater

Walkie Talkie gift!

Chest X-rays on Elf on the Shelf

GPS to grandma's house

gamma	x	uv	infrared	microwave	radio

visible spectrum

Taxonomic classification of
EMPEROR PENGUIN

KINGDOM
Animalia

PHYLUM
Chordata

CLASS
Aves

ORDER
Sphenisciformes

FAMILY
Spheniscidae

GENUS
Aptenodytes

SPECIES
forsteri

common name

SCIENTIFIC NAME

Aptenodytes forsteri

HOW DOES A THERMOMETER WORK?

Electric Thermometer

An electronic thermometer works by detecting the amount of resistance on a strip of metal as the temperature changes.

As metals get hotter, atoms vibrate more inside them, it's harder for electricity to flow, and the resistance increases.

98.6 °F

Liquid thermometer

When the temperature rises, the heat moves from the environment and into the liquid in the bulb causing the liquid to expand.

Either alcohol or mercury

This expansion forces the liquid up the glass tube. The rate of expansion is calibrated on the glass scale in both Fahrenheit and Celsius.

°F   °C

120
100
80
60
40
20
0
20
20

40
30
20
10
0
10
20
30

©@Pinky Science

why do LEAVES change color?

GREEN

Chlorophyll gives plant leaves their green color. In order to produce chlorophyll plants need warm temperatures and sunlight.

YELLOW

As chlorophyll is broken down in Autumn, carotenoids and flavonoids that give plants a yellow color are more obvious.

© Spinky Science

RED

Anthrocyanin (red) is the only color that is made in the leaf. They aren't sure why this happens yet, but they thought that it prevented the leaf from falling off the tree.

ORANGE

Carotenoids are what you see when you see the strong orange color in leaves. Carotenoids breakdown at the same time as chlorophyll, but they do it much slower.

Made in the USA
Coppell, TX
07 November 2024

39775444R10033